BOLEROS

Princeton Series of Contemporary Poets

For other books in the series, see page 97

For other books in the series, see page 97

BOLEROS

/\

Jay Wright

PRINCETON

UNIVERSITY PRESS

Copyright © 1988 by Jay Wright

First published 1991 by Princeton University Press, 41 William Street,
Princeton, New Jersey 08540
In the United Kingdom: Princeton University Press, Oxford

All Rights Reserved

Library of Congress Cataloging-in-Publication Data

Wright, Jay, 1935–
Boleros / Jay Wright.
    p. cm.—(Princeton series of contemporary poets)
ISBN 0-691-06890-9 (acid-free paper) : — ISBN 0-691-01504-X
(pbk. : acid-free paper)
I. Title. II. Series.
PS3573.R5364B6   1991   811'.54—dc20   90-49092

Publication of this book has been aided by a grant from
the Lacy Lockert Fund of Princeton University Press

This book has been composed in Linotron Goudy

Princeton University Press books are printed on acid-free paper,
and meet the guidelines for permanence and durability of the
Committee on Production Guidelines for Book Longevity of the
Council on Library Resources

Printed in the United States of America by Princeton University Press,
Princeton, New Jersey

10 9 8 7 6 5 4 3 2 1

10 9 8 7 6 5 4 3 2 1
(Pbk.)

Designed by Laury A. Egan

For Lois

dyę́ę̨ → la connaissance de l'étoile

loved source of my new words

Acknowledgments

Poems 5, 7, 14, 25, and 39 previously appeared in *Callaloo* #38, Vol. 12, no. 1

BOLEROS

I

I have been considering
how to make of your skill
a holy instance, how
(in other words)
to record the love that turns
a flat white room into
           an aurora australis,
or the cotton shawl
of welcoming light.
That desire requires a skill
quite beyond a poet's art,
something that a word obscures.
Is the touch in your black and gray shawl,
folded so evenly and falling plumb-line
straight from the back of a cane chair,
or in the brown woven wool blanket
smoothed by the foam rubber mattress?
There must be design in the stork-legged
plant in the corner,
or in the wicker basket, cut
and placed to mute the light.
Turn, as my mind does,
through the full ecliptic of your art,
the star still escapes.

When Marcelo comes,
with his water glass demonstration
of overflown friendship,
or Miguel,
picked with the banderillas
of his latest gringa,
or Emilia brings her Homero,
who will cheat at cards,
nothing explains the centered
chime in your voice,

the exuberant stillness
as you rock harmonically
                in your chair.

This globe of a little town goes round
our lives with such swiftness.

Tonight, again,
I will climb the obtuse angled street
to the bodega at the top,
and come back,
sheltering my tortas,
past the open fires of the witches
in the vivienda.
Come back and sit,
with my serrano-laced lomo,
near the soft pearl of your sadness,
and hope somehow to see
                the naked stone.

2

Chaparrita,
morenita
y parece una mexicanita.
How's that for sauce
on your langostinos?

Fish stories.

The gaucharromacho,
singing his liver away
for another love at the next table,
has a factory,
requiring your soonest attention,
                    near Perote.

Stingers,
horned pout,
brown trout.

You should hand him
the bass player Zoom Zoom's card.
Perhaps I'll tell him
how, when you go fishing with our buddy,
I clear one whole room for perch,
another for bass.

Damnable pettifoggers, perch.
Not half so clever as catfish
who can snout bugs out of debris
at the pond's base,
thereby, wise as they are,
giving themselves up to Itzak,
hanging over the emerald water
            above them.

There must be a lesson in that.
There ought at least to be
some applicable homily
in the stance the bass take,
when, gorged on mayflies,
they flicker into the boat
and slowly subside from their feasting,
      and wait greedily for ours.

3

Here we are, disguised in jolly travelers tweed.
No one else seems to mind the fog that must lift
before we do, though we do
and hoe a row of vinyl to the window.
England is a middle age, dark,
bursting with sleeping bags,
                    upon which
the young lie sleeping their halfpenny tastes away,
        if we take this terminal for the terminus
of social form.
And so it dawns at Gatwick,
and we think music would serve
an annunciation, or smooth the gift
of a new sandwich—
thin bread lightly touched with butter,
a sliver of cheese and the coolest cucumbers.

4

Juno, they say, was paler by the yard,
and marble veined,
and sat her veils in a province
other than your Brooklyn.
What do I care?
Mornings I wake to see
your black hair light your pillow,
science enough to start me
roving from a narrow dungeon.
Can Bruno know what you know?
Could Juno have armed her
                    pomegranate touch
with such wisdom, such clairvoyant
attention to my waking?
Could ever betokening Brooklyn have known
what beatitudes I would find
in such a disquieting body?

5

I

All names are invocations, or curses.
One must imagine the fictive event that leads to
He-Who-Shoots-Porcupines-By-Night,
or Andrew Golightly, or Theodore, or Sally.
In the breath of stars, names rain upon us;
we seem never to be worthy.
Or, having learned the trick of being worthy,
we seem never to be prepared for the rein of names,
the principled seating of figures that will walk
beside us, even unto surly death.
Sometimes death has embraced those who never
                              came forth,
those who were impeached for unspeakable desire,
even as they lay in mothers' cave hollow wombs,
speechless, eyeless, days away from the lyrics of light
                              and a naming.
Dead or alive,
something waits in the face or movement
of a child still held in that hollow, something
that will become an appropriate exchange
for the life buried by coming forth, or by
disruption of the life with no reason to appear.
Now, I cannot name the child you carried.
All voices, dilated with need, not desire, have ceased.

II

Each flowered place requires a name that fits.
Fortín de las Flores,
night's cocoa sky, a pond with lightly starred lilies,
gray monastery walls to entice a traveler from discontent,
a skeletal wind (birthmark of a faded desert).

9

Often, when the night has reached its true pitch,
young women in mourning clothes spring up in the garden.
Though it is late, the air sustains mid-afternoon's cilantro,
and the calm prolongs a bell at dusk.
Fortín,
an insupportable garden, a desert bloom,
a flower that offers us its dark solicitude.
I imagine the armor of knowing even its day's
darkness a comfort and the way a singing
seems to arise from cactus too old and too watchful
                                    to be silent.
In the lowlands, I have heard other singing
when, in the middle of the road, the child
asked for water to drink. Now, in the balm of my
heart's double beat, rosemary recovers its essence
and the child commands tonadas alegres, versos elegantes.
These are memory's accoutrements, reason to have searched
a flowered place with a name that fits,
where love's every echo is a child's loss.

III

All names are false.
The soothsaying leaves call winter a paradox—
a northern traveler on a southern wind.
The ice on a weather-broken barn recalls May poppies.
I would have you recall the exhilaration
of reading broken sonnets, on cinnamon-
scented nights, in a tiled room,
while the charity doctors disputed their loves
                        on the cobblestones below.
I enter again the bells and traces of desire,
call and recall, the pacing of love stalking us.
What is love's form when the body fails,
or fails to appear? What is love's habitation
but a fable of boundaries, lovers passing

athwart all limits toward a crux ansata?
I have carried your name on velvet,
knowing you are free, having never suffered
the heartache of patience that love and naming
that this our divided world requires.

6

You will never arrive before these
—the old women who sit
in the rainbow bow of their flower beds,
or the others, strung
near their brace-bound chickens.
It is still worth the blue air,
tucked in your rebozo,
to walk this market's dawn.
Day after day,
you carry the blazon of your string bag
and escape down the same
                    beveled aisles.
I watch you overcome
the saffron song of oranges,
the sapphire trumpet of the sweetest onions.
You resist the bolillo's den dance
and the Salome veil of sugared cakes.
Having found this constant morning
reed voice within you,
you have been informed,
become ancient,
and go only where our necessities
                    lead you.
I, on the other hand,
urge myself toward the lynx-eyed
curanderos who whisper to their
roots and herbs,
or into the bewailing embrace
of cooks whose caustic pots
seem caudle enough for my urges.
So, I go, holding a patch
of wrinkled, penciled paper in hand,
in search of mirto rojo for an ulcer,
or patchless,
pretending to care for ganja.

All who see me read my eyes,
star high with the market's gifts.
Someday, perhaps, I'll learn
how you found the right bank
                 on this peasant's lake
to hear that reed voice, piping the hour
when you might come into the first sun
                 and find yourself alone.

7

Tough old Glasgow tucks itself
            under a leg of the Firth of Clyde.
                    No
Scotia sniveling in that,
just penny-wise prudence, a way
of ladling the elation of coming home.
Logicians on the eastern shore count it
no surprise that queenly old Edinburgh
            lies on the Firth of Forth,
near to the heart of Midlothian.
So, on a doon and windless morning,
we whip east and touch down
near the greenest pasture in Scotland.
As we step from the plane,
the neighboring sheep show us their haggis eyes
            for the flinty spark of a moment.
Suddenly,
I amna deid dune sae muckle as fou,
suspecting that, here, one *can*
thow the cockles o yin's heart,
no small change from a sixpenny planet,
and have the thieveless crony within you
            as suddenly awaken.

We found this bel canto morning
in a Jarocho garden,
on an afternoon when spring had departed
and left only its scunning heat.
I say this now, though I know
that my heart's weather had turned
on a winter night, when I heard the deer
stamping in the water under the raised barn
and felt the star heat fade and the first, clear
cut of loneliness,
the concert pitch of death's tuning.

Marry or burn,
one cannot run away or into,
for there is nothing so sedentary
as the desire to be comforted, by love,
or by some feeling one cannot name.
On Hidalgo, in Guadalajara,
the blue flowers, in their persistence
on the neighbors' white wall,
comforted us, and so the lace of a plaza in sun,
      tacos at dawn from a cart in Gigantes,
the mudéjar ache of the divided cathedral,
the rose pinion of paseos,
              held us till summer.

Those were the garden's traces,
leading to the rose of Midlothian,
the stone house walled in and set
in view of the castle.
Down the road,
the old poet, who did hard times for Lallans,
nests with his chickens and neat Laphroaig.
I count him the most civil of servants,
whose gift is the mist of tongues,
rising from the doom gray of council houses
and snuffed coal mines.
I love the sound of sporran and kilt in his voice,
his refusal to give in to King Street's dovegray manner.

It is some distance to have traveled to learn
to resist being comforted too soon.
Perhaps some moor-stiff night,
we will put on our fog-heavy tweeds
and make our way to old Glasgow,
curled in its water bed,
        confident,
        cocky,
        still uncomforted.

8

Plainly cows normally shit,
but these have been instructed,
and so stand petulantly petered
to have their morning juices sacked.
Don Pepe makes the work a three-minute egg,
brings the bucket of foamy, toast-warm milk
to the patio, where the sugared rum waits in glasses
                              on the leather table.
Stretched taut in leather, we sit to celebrate.
The rum tells us how bright we were to uncover
the rector's night work, to use it to free
your trunks from the docks. Emilia has the story
by halves, her insouciant narrative by the tail.
By the tale, the onyx morning dissolves
into a cream rose afternoon. The lapis lazuli
evening leans lazily on the gate.
Halapa, Chalapa, Shalapa (ever what you call it)
by now has its mist on, and its rain,
with its dew demeanor, clearing the streets.
Lluvia de tontos. Perhaps. And perhaps
two people who have come a long way
welcome the rain screen and the way
the silent evening opens to the night voices,
rising to the terrace of our new home.

9

Nomadic hearts know there is no rose
waiting at every door, that often a threshold's
atmosphere can be worth your life.
Even so, memory must have led us here.

After Perote, the old bus gathers its wings
and swings us through the happy
undulations of fog- and cloud-bound hills,
toward Xalapa, with the cross in its name.
I expect a familiar sand, pillowed against
walls gone red and grainy with heat,
and a muezzin's bell
knitting the loose cloth of evening.
But the heart is a fraudulent voice, a wily ear,
and memory can be too staunchly evangelic.
So the bell goes, in the whisper of matins and vespers,
and the constant idiot's rain dresses the walls
                    in filmy gray.

I should be grateful that memory has left
an anteroom, where I can stock
the cobbled street that leads me to tortillas
and the nuns' diabolic chiles,
or watch the blue-serged licenciado
parade his cane along the Avenida Zamora.
Perhaps I should reserve another room
for the Pérgola's alambres,
and the surpliced children
(hand in hand through the park to school)
and the violet insistence of late afternoon
with coffee and pan on the terrace.
Looking forward, I see the moment
I will choose to leave this garden,
when, on a cloistered morning in April,

I stand in the post office's tiled vestibule
and unlock the rage that you
                    will understand
and a nomadic heart will carry away.

Here,
as we stand in the Mayan evening,
I know I should be able to say
something simple,
such as, it is the same moon,
that the triad—moon, earth,
and that star in Taurus—
sounds right again.
Where is my synodic certainty?
I know less than the ancients
who were accustomed to a late moon
                    and its difficult omens.
Day by day,
from west to east,
the earth rotates on its axis
and the stars,
going against the grain,
shimmy around the one point
                    that seems fixed.
So I know a star stand
when I know where I stand,
linked by that sphere to my own earth.
But these are constant matters,
as measurable as love,
as comprehensible as the heart's ecliptic
you have followed to here.
Some stars neither rise nor set;
some hearts never open.
There is trouble here with the eye,
or the body adapting to a different
                    latitude,
that moment when we know
a star forever invisible,
the body closed upon its own desire.
I am learning,

this deep on the continent,
to remember the Dippers
                 and Cassiopeia,
and to guess at the right linear
constellation,
and the confident moment
when the same moon arrives on time.

11

Down in the lower field,
the doe carcass lies white
on the autumn amber.
This seems to be the end
of the last star-blanched night,
wind sharp with coyotes,
when you felt the deer flow
out of the stream, going
pace by even pace
into the evergreens.
Here, the morning rises,
charged now with a weak sun.
Later, when I return
to stalk birds and darkness
in the evergreens, I
will be as reticent
and serene
as the least of these bones.

a sea calm, cradled by pots at Oshogbo.
You must teach this boy how the long black hair
you used to weave in the water disappeared,
and how your desire created and left him
                    unfinished until the white one came.

Now, the gold air tunes his brass rod body
to the stallion's bell hoof, that voice
we had heard without hearing, and the horse
shudders and begins its patient, memorizing descent.
Twins, whose faces I recognize, lead the tethered horse,
and the nude black woman upon its back flows
into the young man's awakened, dark and Apollonian
                                        embrace.

I4

(CALLIOPE ↔ SAHU)

Night enters the Plaza, step by step, in the singular
flaring of lamps on churro carts, taco stands,
benches set with deep bowls of pozole,
on rugs embroidered with relics, crosses, bones,
                    pamphlets, dream books.
Around this Cathedral, there is an order never shaken;
all our eyes and postures speak of the certainty
                    of being forever in place.
These are the ones who always hear the veiled day fall,
the street tile's serpentine hiss under the evening's drone.
Compadre, not all have come from Reforma, along Madero.
There are those whose spotless white manta tells me
they are not from here—as now, you see, a village
wedding party come to engage the virgin's peace.

This evening, in the Zócalo, lanterns become candles,
or starlight, whatever recalls a woman,
beating her clothes on rocks in a village stream.
At her side, a man buckets the muddy water for his stove.
What does the spirit say, in its seating,
when such impurity can console,
and the slipped vowels of an unfamiliar name
                    rise from the shallows?
Lovers meet here,
and carry consummation's black weed into dawn,
and meet again when the full moon,
                    on its flamboyant feet, surges
over the mud floor of a barrio Saturday night.
She, of the rock, has offered the water man
beans, flour tortillas, cebollas encurtidas, and atole,
a hand for the bell dance that rings all night,
the surprise of knowing the name of the horse
that waits in the shadows when the dance has gone.

She knows this room, where every saint has danced,
revolves on its own foundation,
and that the noon heat ache beneath her hair
guides her through a love's lost steps.
Her love lies deeper than a heart's desire,
far beyond even her hand's intention,
when midnight at the feast sings
with the singular arrow that flies by day,
                    a sagitta mortis.
Now, in her presence, I always return to hands,
parts of that 'unwieldly flesh about our souls,'
where the life of Fridays, the year of Lent, the wilderness,
lies and invites another danger.

I sit at the mass,
and mark the quail movement of the priests' hands,
as they draw submission from us.
The long night of atonement that burrs our knees
                    feeds those hands.
But there are other hands—our own, yet another's—
in the mortar, in the glass,
                    tight with blood and innocence.
A cathedral moment may last for centuries,
given to us as a day, and a day, and half a day,
as a baroque insistence lying over classic form,
as the womb from which the nation rises whole.
Inside there, the nation walks the Chinese rail,
arrives at the Altar of Pardon,
                    lingers, goes on,
to the grotto where the kings stand in holy elation.

Perhaps, this reticent man and woman will find
that moment of exhilaration in marriage, born
on the mud floor when they entered each other
for the good hidden in each, in flesh that needs
                    no propitiation.
There must be a "*Canticle*, a love-song,

an *Epithalamion*, a mariage song of God, to our souls,
wrapped up, if we would open it, and read it."

Adorar es dar para recibir.
How much we have given to this Cathedral's life.
How often we have heard prophecies of famine,
or war, or pestilence, advocacies of labor
and fortune that have failed to sustain.
Compadre, I wish I were clever enough to sleep
in a room of Saints, and close my senses
to the gaming, the burl of grilled meat and pulque,
the sweet talk of political murders, the corrido
laughter that follows a jefe to his bed,
all these silences, all these intimations
of something still to be constructed.
But forgive me for knowing this,
that I have been touched by fire,
and that, even in spiritual things, nothing is perfect.
And this I understand,
in the Cathedral grotto, where the kings have buckled on
their customary deeds, the darkest lady has entered.
Be still, and hear the singing, while Calliope encounters
                                        the saints.
The wedding party,
austerely figured in this man and woman,
advances to the spot where the virgin
                once sat to receive us.

15

(EUTERPE ↔ AB)

In Oaxaca,
women, who speak to no one, carry
boxed hearts from market to market.
Elena brings me a hardwood box,
along with that other life,
now wrapped in manta, and I hear
the river still pecking in the cloth.

Days gone by,
I knelt in the water, in the way of women,
cradling a grief that could only be named
                        by going away.
I remember
I saw the river pull its drying legs together,
and heard some thing, or someone, cut
a dark path through the trees near the shore.
I imagined the god had gone to ground,
and that river stones would then dull
                        and grow silent.
I, myself, was a boy in a box,
            cradle or coffin,
and the voice I heard above me
dressed me in despair.
                        Moment to moment,
my limbs and spirit grew to fit my Iroso boat.
I had no idea that I would follow
an Indian stream to Manhattan,
and be bereft of the skill to escape from,
or to live within, my heart's box.

Life in this place has taught me to scamp love;
therefore, I find it easy to sail Manhattan's
watercourse,
            with Elena,

though her eyes are rose gardens of injuries,
and her voice shakes the dry bean of Oaxaca
                                    within her.
I know her heart is a double flute,
and that the blue mountain she left,
above the starched plaza,
is truly made of water,
and that the gift she brings in the hardwood box,
rests, awaiting the bone flute sound
                    of my washed desire.

16

(THALIA ↔ KA)

It is simple to ache in the Bone, or the Rind.
Sit here with me, near this solitude.
Sweet black coffee and pan close the heat out.
Down below, ship lights
bubble up and bob on the water.
The chains being dropped into the water ring bells,
recalling the anklets the city wore,
when it danced both day and night.

We then dressed in the finest sunspun white clothes.
No corner in the Villa Rica de la Vera Cruz
lay without lovers, or ambition,
memory and precept of the soul's discovery
in coffee, tobacco, bananas, sugarcane,
and cattle still steaming through the cool moments.
The city was a soul admitted to itself.
Blessed and spirit warm,
it flew from wall to wall, to feed upon
funeral offerings of meat, cake, and beer.

Some of us had been once removed,
and had gone north of the Cuban vowel,
the dropped consonant,
                              to arrive
on the fortunate side of the double face,
to affirm the heart's education
                    in leaving home, to arrive
fulfilled with the same desire.

I met my twin on a mountaintop,
in an ancient theater, in a new world,
where the black-robed turns and counterturns
involved me in a dream of a polar privacy.

I could then speak of happiness
                a child could understand,
and rub shoulders with a grace,
                descended from a mother,
who had often given birth to despair,
and had laid it in the weed of her solitude.

Come sit here, now, with me, in this solitude,
and teach me to hear the song
I have composed,
and teach me the reason why
I avoid so narrowly
                my fidelity.

Double heart on a double journey,
I ache, in the bone and rind,
to enter the mask that guides my eyes
from a dead thing to a green bird,
opening its sail into a greener forest.

I 7

I awaken to the silver spur bells and ecstasy of a city
                              astride the sun.
My eye chooses a narrow path.
In the rose dark, I see a sannyāsin arise,
set his pot upon the ground and, shedding
his flayed orange skin, step into the Ganges.
Black spirits such as mine will always come
to a crossroads such as this, where the water moves
with enabling force, and the body snuggles
in the arms of a weightless mother
                              who will not let go.

My mother travels the night sky,
in the light of a sacred rose, and rides
a lotus blossom that shines with the "unbroken
                              light of heaven."
She has become the center of her own mandala,
Kāśī itself, seated upon a trident above the earth
                              that sustains her.
She was,
when the world began,
a heron who clutched the conical stone
as it pierced the receding water at dawn.

"Dawn is the sacred hour in the City of Light."
Now, when morning unwraps the Age of Strife, and lays it
in the crimson mud heat of the Rio Grande,
I enter the water again,
to uncover a visible heart,
to hear the mother's tale of a woman surging
out of a brass pot, over this desert.
How can I be made by John a watchful spirit,
a water boat, when the water I enter
is shell and vision of a god's body,

spring of a devotion without book?
Sun cannot save us, skull bearers,
scourged by memory and the great vow,
even when the vessel in our hands turns
                              on its axis from darkness into light.
Day by day,
my skull cup fills with a longing,
a desire to see that black virgin queen,
enthroned with the child in her lap,
or a woman made whole through a Śiva dance,
and the morning clarified by meditation.

This skull I carry is wet with ashes,
tea leaves I read in back rooms, in leaky
houses, at the end of dirt roads, lined with sycamores—
leaves which recall an exalted nest, with the bird voice
                                            fading away.
Why should I carry this coffin, this pillar
from the childbearing tree, and out of the cradle
endlessly rock my sarco-phagus self?
Pandās, when they speak, remind us of the way the city
peels away, layer by layer (Kāśī,
                  Varāṇāsī,
                        Avimukta)
until we reach the stone in its heart,
and the blossoming well of bliss.
The soul walks Kāśī,
spins its fibrous body, then plunges
into the light of a water so deep it has
                              disappeared.
When I walked away from the cathedral passion of slave markets,
free at last,
my bones were dressed by the wind,
my breath danced in a cavern
where I had held a universe of vision and desire,
death and its imaginative discipline,
life, with its intensive and aged compassion.

I knew my heart a flayed thing,
unable to contain the tīrtha glow that would light me
                                              to another.

No ship on the sea of night waited.

Like the god I had many faces,
but mine were unfamiliar, singular,
rope tense and edged with poverty.
For the death of the seed within me,
I thought I would anoint myself
with ashes from a funeral pyre.

So I travel from life to life with these God thoughts,
in a time of vision, having put away all hope,
having undone my freedom in meditation,
in austerity, in sacrifice,
yet with my work-instructed hands spinning
                the jeweled beads of the spirit's life.
This bead ticking calls me back to Kāśī
and the bronze gleam of water on these pilgrims' backs.
There I go, swaddled in white, strapped to a bamboo litter.
Lifted up, I arrive on the last ground,
slide into the gray water and rise to assume my pyre.
That son, invested with his age and seamless white,
transports the fire, circles me.
I flame again in his last embrace.
I will be blind to his indifference
when he bathes my gathered form with water
from a clay pot, and walks blindly away.
I will sleep on the water,
and hear no mourning, no lamentation.

But I have slept before in an invested tree,
and solicited the wine succulence of the women's
                                        grieving voices.
I was once a scholar,
who, following the bee buzz of a Maya text,

left my Arizona orange groves for the shag cut
and tensile heat of Jalisco, and there I died.
Huichol men who had seen me pass—
             morning after morning, night after night—
who had dipped their heads in coffee cups
and day-old newspapers when I greeted them,
sent their wives to exult in their common grief.
I followed that text to the cottonwoods in Mississippi.
                          And there I died.
I stood apart from my breath-emptied form,
while men in black and women in white
rode the waves of their grave fitted voices
to my bier, and tossed their nickels and dimes into it,
                          for my burial.
Out of the cradle, into the nest,
onto the cross, and into the ship of the dead,
by the light of a great lamp,
I moved by degrees toward a still center,
able to deny my rising and falling,
able to inhabit my many hearts
and to accept my soul's singular involution.

My day continues.
I must now go down to the water
to hear the phrase that binds me to the truth within me.
Who will sit with me at the water's edge
to retell the story of my devotion,
to celebrate the careful way I have stepped around
             every holy moment
to fix my mind on auspicious things?
Who will understand how willows and their water roots,
Guinea hymns, guilt and fear turned me,
burdened by a sacred thread,
away from the sight of my North Star,
made me unable to take even seven fraudulent
             steps toward my liberation?

Here, in Banāras, my day continues.

Having entered the city,
I thought the dark one had cut my defiance
and self-mutilation away from me.
I know now I am no longer perfect.
I decide to approach only the twilight water,
and to take my ash-filled cup,
against all assurances, to offer an invitation,
and to retain the power to thread a skein
of injury from my life.
Even in Kāśī,
I cannot ask for the white depth of forgetfulness.

Follow me,
as autumn throws its crisp haze over the uncut fields.
Old wood—poplar, pine, ash, beech, some birch—
has been tumbled, and stacked in the near corner
of the nearest field.
Tonight, the slim moon leans on the hill.
So still, we can hear the bear snuffling
around the dying apple trees,
and the baying of an old man at his well.
Surely,
here is the cabbage smell of peace,
the venison taste of an earned happiness.
Kāśī, clamorous and brassy with its silks and bronze cups, lies.
I lie, when I extol a moment that shows us we are alone.

Still, I have my devotion.
And perhaps only the skull bearer knows
how devotion, the water urge that cut us
from the fire altar, binds us to a new land.
When, tonight, under a new moon,
the soul's calendar turns another page,
I will go down, ash laden, and walk
the transforming light of Banāras.

18

(POLYHYMNIA ↔ KHAIBIT)

When the light struck me,
the hostile road grew calm.
I heard my name, tintinnabulating
in the desert air,
and felt the sea spray of fear in my belly.
How could I have been blind when I saw so clearly
what the others had been denied?
And how can I explain how the enharmonic
rapture of my name left them deaf?
Perhaps, at that moment,
they shivered with their Whitsun agues,
arrogant as ever with their baskets of first fruits.
But death, the potter, had given me a new vessel,
and I shook it before their eyes
                        though they were blind.
I needed Ananias to make sense
of the blood I now carried with me,
and when he swaddled me with the white water,
my bull roarer voice released the rising song in me.

Buried, therefore,
I remember the flowering water
and how it lifted my ship,
            the *Flor de la Mar*,
out of its solitude,
and prepared me
to bring forth an obedience of faith.
How did I know then that that very boat
would become my coffin, my cross,
the shadow my name would wear
under a new dispensation?

I write these letters to people who distrust me,
and assure them I admire their evangelical successes.

I wish I could forget my own successes,
the days I spent beating the scrabbling Roman pilgrims
                    away from their convictions.
No one forgives me for showing love's failures.
Yet I know that love awakens grace in the one
                              who struck me.

I remember the flat curl of the road,
the mangy dogs scurrying away from us,
the round silver tray of the sun,
          as it slipped out of a cloud's pocket.
My only defense against the enticing cloth
of the women's voices
was to count the steps I had taken.
But now that I lie on this Teotihuacán bed,
only the mathematics of my ascent to here
                              concern me;
only the singular obsidian urge
that obliterates the trinity in me
                    brings me any peace.
Yet when the knife's glaze surrounds my heart,
I plunge, and plunge again,
into a desert river,
          where cross and coffin and shadow
compose my mother's absence,
and raise the anchored ship of my life
from body to house to spirit,
into the recognition of a sea deep need
                    my death commands.
I glow with this necessary entry.
And every entry is "a circumcision of the heart by the Spirit."

I should have written my life on cave walls,
and shut it away from light
                    and falling breath,
held it free of the crafty penumbra
                    of my New Spain dáma.
You then would have had to sit in my cave,

and light juniper twigs
to burn ox fat in a limestone cup,
and watch Affonso play among his many disguises.
I am that Affonso who found some comfort
in the purl of rails and cactus,
the silent skid of white pine out of the Zuñi mountains,
the crisscross of Aztec lives that waited for me here
                    when my king abandoned me.

Sea green birds, hungry after their flight,
peck at the new morning in me,
and the nine syllables of Egyptian desire
                    spell my ancient name.
I must learn the dialectic of love's form
in the call that came with the light,
and live with the three-petaled rose of my new name,
                    here, in this new world.

19

(CLIO ↔ KHU)

In my Biṅu shrine, the sọgọ altars pull me home.
The stone I lay upon on Teo found itself
in a dance of stones,
four sisters turning near a brown pond,
each a promise of the sea within me.
For years now, Bamako has been dry.
Millstones,
        which held Nommo's
                and the rain gods' gifts,
fade into the bilious doors.
Nevertheless,
the bilu still whisper in spirit ears,
and my father seeds my spirit
              with the first fruits of autumn,
pots that address the dead in me.
Yet I know myself an "intangible ethereal casing,"
lucent intelligence,
heavenbound by being bound to the emblems
                  of my person.
Clio call me,
scroll of the brave,
with one foot in the bush,
            one foot in the city,
a human tongue fit for taunting
the pretensions of pure love,
and an ear for the wind sound of a woman
riding a seashell into this desert desolation.
Though I have second sight,
my creations wither and die.
The balance I found easy escapes from my gardens.
I continue to weave my checkerboard,
cloth of the Word,
healing music of the head,
my soul's improvisation.

(*Art Tatum*)

       When I sit at the piano,
       I don't count the keys.
       I see you looking at my eyes;
       you wonder what I see.
       What I see is in my touch,
       and in the assurance
       that the sound will be right there.
       Some cats always carp.
       They say the music isn't mine,
       keep asking me for "an original."
       So I lay two notes in the bar ahead,
       diminish a major,
       tunnel through the dark
       of the brightest minor,
       and come out on the right side of the song.
       I pick the composer's pocket,
       and lay the hidden jewels out there.
       This wired, hammering woman
       wants her fortune told.
Hammer and anvil guide the music of my house,
smithy of the ear's anticipation, forge
of the mind in what it denies
            and what it fulfills.
On the terrace,
altars resonate with the water sound
of goatskin over hollow wood,
and the frog pitch of the mudbanks
within the house
            answer.
I dream of the smith music within me,
and hear its cithara voice in the dyēli's craft.

20

(TERPSICHORE ↔ SEKHEM)

"The night has a tree / with amber fruit; /
            the earth has an / emerald hue."
Late, by Waverley Station,
Edinburgh draws its foggy curtain.
We et our mixed grills and hotpies
in a blue forest of a room that stood
at the head of the stairs on St. Andrew.
Wilson walks me from the bus station,
to which he will return,
                threading the maze of the summer's fog.
When we arrived this afternoon,
we saw St. Christopher sitting alone and stoned
                        on the still bus to Lanark.
We would have invited him into the puzzle
of our afternoon,
but his Kāla Bhairava eyes kept us away.
No loss. No reason to remember
the Pentland flax and tweed that warm his tongue
when he sits in the Edinburgh dock.
Furies dance for the three of us
            with a Dumfries list,
and, even though I click my cowries,
I hear the Dionysiac thiasus lag
            at the Castle gate.
That "changes the image /
            but not the virginity of its daring."

Ramón laid his anguish in heaven,
squeezed a grieving waltz from amber earrings
            and jasmine in a woman's hair.
But perhaps even here in Edinburgh,
we share that same "bruma de invierno,"
and fall out of control into a Celtic dance—

beat and counterbeat where the ambush occurs,
sleepless nights following the rhythm
                              of a seed in love.
I imagine St. Christopher set spinning in New Town,
and his turn and counterturn reinventing
a flaming solitude, burning a heron dream
                              grown truly dark.
Even such a dream has its arid corner,
an appleless neighborhood,
withered by desire and ambition.
In the Zócalo,
a red candle under a cross sits
to remind us of a stellar mask
                    that dawn on Teo recalls.

Every dance is convivial,
just as the pipes and beers we share,
waiting here for the train to take me away.
The absent one gives our love shape,
dresses our "dreams in indigo, our joy in gold."
I know you will not accept that form alone is empty.
            No se cumple, no se cumple,
                    my teacher sings.

"Llevo tantas penas en el alma."
What is the obstinate death without end?
What can be spoken when the bird falls away
from the fullness of its song?
What memory governs loss,
                sekhem of solitude,
                Huichol eye into bliss?
Under the amber Edinburgh night,
the singing mask arrives,
The-One-Who-Comes-in-Good-Time,
precursor of the Cool World.
"Nada puedo entender ni sentir sino a través de la mujer."

"Power made visible."

I staunch you now in faith's blackness,
a compassion that being strange revives
and secures.

2 1

(URANIA ↔ REN)

Letter by letter,
the Villa Real de Santa Fé de San Francisco
                              fades away.
It would have been better
for the village to withhold its name,
and to lie in the arms of the Sangre de Cristo
and dream only of the healing oil in myrtle.
But the city has grown out of its rose and dove shape,
become an abiku, with bells for the war in its spirit.
Santa Fé no longer hears its dolphin voice,
or the bronze stroke of Mali emblems,
marking the road from region to village
          to this rosewood door in my adobe wall.
Santa Fé seems always to be rising and falling,
seems always amidst a turtle walk
                    toward its own body,
always ready to embrace the figure
that reveals its incompleteness.

We had escaped from the pagan nets
set low in the two rivers,
had struggled, and landed on the high ground
of Pueblo faith,
and there set down, where those
with drier hearts had abandoned the sun.
Yet faith requires a larger globe than this plaza,
and more water than the bishop's bronze cup
                              can hold.
When the faithful plunged into the Rio Grande,
toward Guadalupe,
I dressed myself in their cloth,
burned their crops, and sat clear-eyed
in their churches, waiting
                    for my name to appear.

45

That was an informative loss,
one in which the mussel shell of devotion
would draw my groin's heat
                    down,
into the forgotten water of orisha love.
I lost the city again,
traded in sheep, wool, wine, and pelts,
learned how an unknown apple
                    had been my only globe,
the formal star shine of a face I could not put on.

Now my trade is dust.
But my name has retained an immaculate dew,
drawn from waterless places.
In my stolen forest,
Odomankoma guides Urania's hand
through the formalities of a house,
where love's formal body has set its passion.

SAINTS' DAYS

22

NUESTRA SEÑORA DE LA PAZ (JANUARY 24TH)

At the upper end of this continent,
along the St. Lawrence,
one has to learn to live with winter,
a wood cat with a devouring patience
and a tempered ear for the softest harmonics
                              of resignation.
Some of us call it an affordable peace,
and tuck the winter in journals
that stand hip to hip with rose bibles,
and string, on midwinter rosaries,
our spring weariness.
Hour to hour,
coquettish January sits in our warm rooms,
undresses, draws near and caresses
                    the longing within us.
Strange to think of such a virgin,
drawing a midwinter veil over our hearts,
and trying to sound the enharmonic note
that will distinguish peace from death.

23

NUESTRA SEÑORA DE LOURDES (FEBRUARY 11TH)

Morning memories take root in me,
here, a winter away from New England.
I solve the maze of milk and papaya,
coffee and sweet bread, the new black cigar
laid on a silver dish next to my coffee cup.
Doña Ana, on her way to the cathedral
on Zaragoza, just before the Hotel Salmones,
                                        nods.
I drop her mild satisfaction
into my own honey jar of contentment.
Black, they say, she wears black days about her;
no sun lights them.
I have seen, on certain rainy Saturday nights,
women, who speak no Spanish, emerge
from the shadowed tiles,
with limping or dazed familiars
clutched to their breasts, curtsy
and enter through her figured door.
A year in this city has given me
a thirst for the waters of that basilica,
and the courage to walk the bridge
                of the silence she displays.
Peasant ears like hers, I know,
can hear the spring beneath the grotto.
Her voice glows with the rainbow of passion
that speaking to holiness must disclose.
She stands, in her bones, giving evidence
of the bhakti of suffering.
I know that, if I could go beyond
that figured door, I would see her walls,
figured with every victory
                        over such suffering.
I speak the words now,

by which I fortify myself against
the left hand of my person,
and recall that the Lady sits
on the left bank of the Gave de Pau.
Promptly, this morning, the rain begins to fall.
The spring New England promised comes
                              to sit at my side.
And in the stillness the rain draws from us,
I seem to hear Doña Ana begin her prayers.

24

SAN JUAN DE DIOS (MARCH 8TH)

Today,
in San Juan,
winter turns a scarlet eye upon us.
Dry rain slides down a dry amber path.
I should be gone.
But I have nestled the wind in my beard,
and lifted my head to the feather voice
of a stricken bird within me.

Now the day doubles at my feet.

It is always at this hour
that I recall the exhilarated,
red Sunday moment,
when the cross lowers another bull
to the gray, exhausted Mexican earth.

25

SAN ANSELMO (APRIL 21ST)

Who will say he saw me
when I lit the twin tapers
of those cottonwoods near the river,
or knelt, with my face in muck,
to hear the bull roar of locusts?
Those who knew me then
knew I had been given
                    the vernacular of streams.
But, though the cottonwood blaze lit
an envy in the valley for the crux in my person,
I had no wish to be holy
                    nor any need for devotion.

I had come from Tepic,
with a Huichol graininess so deep within me
it lingered on my breath.
I lied to those around me about dove-headed gulls,
rose purple water at Vera Cruz,
moons strung full and radiant
                    above sunless noon plazas.
I carried, in a goat hide pouch,
the secret day of my naming.

So prophecy, without my consent,
followed me, and took me in hand.
I grew rich under the Gaulish peat
and Celtic chamois that buffed my Roman name.

But I go too fast.
Gradually, the fermented milk of liturgy
claimed me; I read myself into stupors.
My mother ground the red corn of my absence,
and washed me away.

My father hired a wanderer,
a vagabond, a slave, if you wish,
to walk beside his oxcart in my place.
No one, in the high airs of a deserted village,
chose to remember me,
or the nasal explosion of my name.

I went further away.
I followed an Augustine, or Agustín,
through the Florida everglades.
I knew him then as one who had come
                hard tack- and callous-laden,
                        out of Fort Smith, Arkansas.
He walked with a wave-like limp,
a result of the chains they bestowed upon him,
further south,
for the black Baptist challenge in his flute voice.
This, I told myself,
would be my pandit, arguing with a river darkness,
my dyēli, lifting the prayer from a harmattan life.

I say, those who know
know I would be ruled by faith,
but that I profess nothing,
and have no anodyne for the spasms
                of a speechless heart.
Why else should my heart have led me
out of Piedmont, to Bec,
where I would learn to speak
                of blessedness and grace?
Why should I now be sailing
the backwaters of these slave sabbaths
to dispute salvation with those who have
                the book by ear?
Why should I suffer Gaunilo's tone-deaf carping,
when I sound my soul's perfect triad?

Still I go on,
past the moment in the Zócalo,

when the bitter pozole of doubt
fell into my bowl,
past the moment when I furled
my Burgundy credo, and drifted
past the dock of God's name,
past the ship's bell of Agustín's
                                singular love.
The fool has said,
            I desire to understand.

It is far too easy to be left alone.
I learned to speak simply,
while others raised willows
around their words, and to lead
those who would pick a simple dandelion
through the oak and hickory forest
                        of my own words.
And so, by degrees, I packed my solitude,
my desert father's inclinations,
my hawk-headed urgencies,
my Mixteca discontent,
and brought them to the water
my faith would stir into rapture.

Standing in the gold mosaic of a forest wall,
my heart promised me an eternity.
Still, I saw a white depth,
a blank arch in my faith's house.
What but a promise could I be?
What, when I turned my soul-heated eyes
upon the forest's cross, could I see
                        but emptiness?
I knew then,
in spite of my mind's heavy parchment,
that I could prove nothing.
That morning, surely, you remember
I reached into the brazier of my devotion
for the fire I took to the cottonwood tapers,
lit them, and lay down in the ultimate flare

of a moment, when someone
might have seen and dressed my spirit's
naked body.

26

CORPUS CHRISTI (MAY 25TH)

So the White Sunday,
when the real presence of love
is possible, passes,
and mud heat rises once again
in the red hours,
field hours, recalled
in the faint trembling of cowbells.
Life here is so level
a quick spray of fireflies at dusk
comes as a starburst over July.
In such an atmosphere,
some live on visions,
the bloodstained marble of an altar,
devotion to a boned body that has
a king proceed by candlelight
amidst a flag flying of trades,
                a clamor of crafts.
        At Kāśī,
        in the Vishvanātha temple,
        a worshipper approaches darśana
        with a joyful noise,
        and you can hear the surge of that river,
        as it rises and falls
        here in the sabbath air.
But what are days but the soul's definition
                      dominicae trinitatis,
moments that arrive veiled,
a question of number and the absolute IS,
which is, in Jerusalem, a bride?
I tell you there are only three festive
moments in a life,
each a seed dancing in a wayward mistral.
Ask me for evidence.

I tell you,
in Liège, I saw
Bedouin-draped nuns circle
the festering hide of a Trinity Sunday,
and heard a kora ecstasy
                    still vibrating within them.
Even in blue-stockinged Rome,
those who had tolle'd and legge'd with the saint
felt a discontent when they were belled at last
to bed, and rose, with a peasant Pope,
quarreling with serenity.
But the temple will not open its sabbath door
                              to such delight,
except on Thor's day, a jovial, perhaps,
market day, thick with omens and oaths.

I will open a temple,
where joy becomes more than a body
raised and pressed to a penitent's tongue,
though I know that love must remain
                    festum of and in the body,
and a plainchant for a rude southern evening,
when work is the name I take
                    and most adore.
There, when the Real Presence defies me,
the blue lamp of a forest spirit leads me home.

27

SAN PEDRO / SAN PABLO (JUNE 29TH)

"Last of all, as to one untimely born, he appeared to me."

There are moments when I wish that my mother
had less of the book by heart,
and that the sugar bowl of her faith
                              were sometimes dry.
Who wants her spicy saint's eye
following you into the plaza's dark and curiously
curled corners,
after you have left the dance in your neighbor's stall,
and gone currying for the love thorns on Nicolasa's body?
And who wants to hear her voice,
exalting the coverlet of a light blue morning sky,
while you, fastened in the pinafore of your petate bed,
toss in a faceless novia's arms?
It is enough that she imagines that this lake
is Bethsaida, or Galilee, and that the rock hard
sustenance she finds in you grows
from the temple bell voice you've heard,
calling you away from your exhausted nets.

But so, my name was given by my arrival
in summer's first heat,
and by my mother's understanding
that what is sown dies and comes to life,
love's seeded protestation,
the spirit's rehabilitation after it has denied itself.
And yet, when I stand and pull the radiant fish
from Ajijic, I feel the Pauline tension in my body.
I know this day holds a double blessing,
and perhaps it would have been better
for my mother to conceive,
and to bear upon this very day,

a second gifted child, too diffident to deny
                the authority in my name.
I would have had reason then to argue
with her need to lament the withered fig tree
of her body, her desire
to extol the conversion of a rejected stone,
into a riverworn altar,
or into a sun calendar,
                turning of its own weight.
And, though this lake lies distant from every gate
my mother's heart has entered,
to prepare me to hear the divinity in my calling,
and to see at the end of sun-benumbed days
the Lazarus light of this Mexican soil,
I would have welcomed the star-fall of suffering
her life had promised me.

Now, I go slowly over the rock of my name,
touching the water-smoothed edges,
listening for the cock crow in my spirit,
the threefold betrayal of my mother's grace.

"Why am I in peril every hour?"

If he has appeared to Simon,
it is by the grace of God I am what I am
and the desert light becomes lake light.
The saints have married.
And my mother will call me Peter,
and ask me again to "speak to the people
                all the words of this Life."

28

SANTA CRISTINA (JULY 24TH)

Even then the cypresses were dying,
and olives rarely raised their black heads at our tables.
Prophecy had given us that Dalmatian slave,
with god's mark in his name, an Imperator and a Dominus.
Maximian fixed us in the yoke,
while *he* rose golden from the cocoon,
silk-webbed in his own importance,
weaving preferments and new houses in his flight.
If he had been born to more than tolerance,
patience and strength in his own ambition,
faith's river would have flowed smoothly at Bolsena,
and the Anicii would sit fat and undisturbed.

I wish they had given you a name such as this:
      María Christina Henrietta Désirée Félicité Rénière.
Though yours is hidden there,
I can't be sure of yours—Barbara? Catherine? Ursula?
The Austrian walked, by renunciation, into Spain;
you walked, through destruction, into the silence
                            around your name.
Loss and double loss.
The person gone through the house's door into death,
the body gone through marriage and, finally, death.
Passage into passage, what remains of you
shows in an intimation of loss, or in faith's intimacy.
So your head rests on the high altar of the Milan cathedral,
and your heart in the House of the Noble Ladies of Saint Theresa.

In a saint's body, familial hegemony breaks down.
Or, in one who remembers the saint and dresses in spirit,
the body, buckled against Carlists and banners that flare
the sky with a strange trinity, decomposes.

Where could you be found apart from an enclosure?
How could you retain even the hint of your name,
                                    except in retreat?
Saint and regent, you move out of the world.
Father gone.
Diocletian gone.
Isabella gone.
The monarchy shapes itself again;
God's many voices fashion redemption's wheel,
but nothing saves you, for no one sees you.
Even Cranach and Veronese, lifting a hymn
from a millstone, pincers and afflicting arrows,
disguise you,
and the sharp castanets of a Catalan night
only recall your double loss and your spirits'
twin passage into a sacrifice you must return
                                    to renounce.

29

SANTA CLARA (AUGUST 12TH)

(*crucifix*)

Clara   Agnèse   Ortolana   Beatrice
             Di Favarone
The knight's disposition fails; an order falls.
The first to move is light. Love's intelligence invades her,
and the silver moonlight of the Gammadion, or the tau,
draws her into cloistered space, where the family
                         begins to reinvent itself.
If sullen Constantine, browbeaten by a vision, knew anything,
he knew his mother's story,
how she was led by the Palestinian to dig, just at that spot,
for the crosses and the nails; how the injured woman
was stretched upon the proper boards and rose
                         with a dance in her body.
So the legend reinvents the form of suffering
and the exuberance of discovering what time,
or another hand, had buried,
and you, who now require light's investment
in cloistered figures,
embrace the familial strangeness that the book alone
                                    can give.

(*lily*)

After the sackcloth and alms, comes marriage.
In love's white lace, you approach Portiuncula,
through a curtain of candlelight,
there where the altar promises you excision
and its own chaste obedience to the light within you.
How full you appear, λείριον, in that invested darkness;
how, like the red lily's, your spirit toils, unappeased
by the rumor and thrust of red robes in your life.

Say that an Eastern austerity shaped you from Hera's milk,
and that the spring's cuckoo has taught you the wrong passion,
or that the tense brown field you inhabit leads your heart
                                        astray,
toward ecstasy and a devotion you disguise
                        as absolute penance.
I know you by another,
the name wedded to the cross,
the voice encouraged by the many gifts
                        acquired through suffering.
Yet such suffering never releases Aphrodite's rose,
and both the rose and the suffering you disdain.
        Your tempered life leads toward a different order,
                        and the clarity of rule.

(book)

He refuses
—through Assisi indolence or excessive love—
he refuses the book upon which your heart is set.
You have only the Form of Life and the Last Will,
pentatonic scales for which no composition calls,
black marks inadequate to devotion's choir within you.
We are talking now about need,
and every reason to recall how, out of the huts,
they wander two by two, ragamuffins
more comfortable with prayer than with the Book,
patched souls who refuse money's hard and liberating
                                        touch,
God's jongleurs, lifting an evangelical hymn from labor.
We are talking now about initiation, and the way
a double mind looks at the red chapel of the book,
and flees, toward sacrifice,
and the dissolution of its own claims.
How could he write you out of your intuition
and into the keeping of love's hearth-seeking candle?
How could he place your name near the blue vowel of loss?
The book now rests on a lotus blossom.

Words have been changed.
You retreat.

(*ciborium*)

Death in the deep awaits the Great Mother.
Death in the water lily.
Death in the cup suspended over the altar.
What is the domestic day to the altar?
What covered chalice can contain
life's unequivocal ascent and descent,
the spring flowing and returning
                    to its own enclosure?
I must tell you
that wisdom sits, circled by star silver blossoms,
on a lotus chair, under a canopy of light.
She is that canopy,
the great lamp on the sea of night,
wood of the hieros gamos,
suffering bed of the awakening
                  and of the going away.
He now would step down,
leave the garden's tending to Elias, leave you the rule.
How unlike the vessel to disappear,
to deny the creative wood of a heart returning
                        to itself.
Still your passionate lily flowers by the altar,
enraptured by its austerity, enthroned
                  by its own seclusion.

30

NUESTRA SEÑORA DE LOS REMEDIOS (SEPTEMBER 24TH)

"When they came to my house that night
the dog barked twice, and the old man got up
and went out of doors and then came back and lay down;
she flew out again, and I got up and went out of doors;
I knew the slut barked more than usual,
but I could see nothing; I went back into the house,
and just as I got into bed five men bulged right
against the door, and it fell right in the middle of the floor,
and they fell down."

They fall before James and San Ramón,
with their vows and an urge to be useful;
they move in the waters of an old text.
Such piety turns on a name change
        —Pity, Mercy, Ransom—
and under the spin of a different star
                becomes Remedios.

Remedios.
Time now to reconstruct salvation.

They have come to take back their losses; they fall,
and thrust their hands into the night's cowl,
a caul for the woman's devotion to her offensive husband.
What can that lunar memory tell them about their failings?
What can their white hoods conceal, except the moment
when the sheared soul chose to cover its face,
and tuned its voice to a withered heart's power?
                Hannah will testify,
        "In the red times, how many times have
        they took me and turned my clothes

over my head and whipped me?
I do not care what they do to me now
if I can only save my land."
In Hannah's life,
Remedios sutures her vindication in the earth,
and the morning upon which her melon seed begins
its slow descent into life, Hannah sings.
But here in the dark,
her eye lights a disfigured tree,
and remembers the river beneath that cross.
Death rises from that supple water,
and washes over the firstborn among the dead.
What do these five men, trying to circle
their stumbling shadows in a shattered cabin,
know about that one Who is the Beginning, who is
a verb change that opposes self-possession?
What can they take away,
when the woman's assurance has dispossessed them?
And so, for no reason, they wait.

Who here, even in the heart of the Vera Cruz, remembers that river?

The burnt brown edge of coffee in the air
inaugurates Wednesday near Consolapa.
The small waterfall breaks over the smooth stones
under the bridge,
where Doña Elpidia, with an eye on me,
thrashes and mauls her manta in the white water.
In the distance, a hummingbird catches a phrase
from the stream, and sends it spiraling
                              over the chestnut trees.
September has spread its peace between the woman and me.
The sun lingers.
Elpidia sets a star of stones on the bank,
and stretches her wet clothes there to dry.
Elpidia, the water, the frayed clothes
cradle me now in their chronometry.

On the old house's water-stained walls
I still see visions.
At night, the flat leaves of the cactus
in the patio become palms upon drums.
Witches know me.
And Elpidia knows my need to embrace
the bull's horn in their voices,
or the silence when they are gone.
Late September recalls Elpidia to her saint's day,
to the feast of her own flowering in sacred water.
In New England now, the leaves are already auburn-haired,
and the Herefords have begun to huddle against the intimation
of the first snow.
I have followed the earth's spine out of the White Mountains,
and have leapt, by my own impulse, away from a familiar
body, to here, where Doña Elpidia has shown me
the left side of solitude.
In the water's froth, she wrings out her losses:
a son in the cotton near Bakersfield; a husband
scrabbling in Guatemala; a gachupín daughter in Perote;
the stranger in the holy house by the stream,
who hides his eyes until she looks away.
A mile away, she keeps her hectored cattle
moping in the stringy grass,
and waits for her silence to invite me home.
I wake, sweat-cold, in midnight's brightest light,
shawl myself in gray, and take my first step
toward her adobe house.
I breathe with the stream's breath,
as I go up and against it.
Darkness lays its red crown on her land.
I continue,
up, where I will fall, and be unable
to promise more than my own vindication.

Rhythm rules, even when the darkness covers us.
Spirit's clock measures the self's repossession.

Five men, intent only upon a killing, ease themselves
into Hannah's dark.
                    They will not be comforted.
They will not understand how the cradle breaks,
and how the ship she keeps on the sea of night
                        sails away from them.
Death here is the ultimate refusal,
the search for redemption's new name, the verb
that only Hannah hears and will learn to spell.

        Mendicant, I flow as the river flows,
        seeking the pledge of fulfillment.
        I hear the hidden tone in Elpidia's name,
        and see, for a moment, the act
                        that name elicits.
        Green water under a green tree responds
        when I call into her house.

SAN RAFAEL ARCÁNGELO (OCTOBER 24TH)

Enoch, I walk about the earth the *angels* have defiled.
Strange, that, in this high valley, summer rain
at four in the afternoon clears the Alameda air.
                    Perpetuamente Osanna sverna,
as now out of my cave I climb,
an educated bear, marshing through solitude's mud springiness.

I see him turn out of Dolores, and come toward me.
I recognize him as one who keeps the nickel dances,
down along San Juan, alive by day.
But early evening sweeps him, a twisting leaf,
along Juárez and into the park, where he fastens himself
                    to an old bench or a trouser leg.
My turn to read his book—
the tattered bracero breviary passed from Empalme,
through Tepic and Atotonilco, to here.
I know the story as a water legend,
made miraculous and difficult by being true.
We take the city's slowly kindling streets,
                    smoking, spitting the sour fish taste
of words we will not say into the gutters.
                    God heals, he tells me.
Why should this limping peon believe in a book
he knows, if at all, only by ear or by hearsay?

In Bernalillo, above Albuquerque,
a curandero has his own disguise, a hobbled shepherd,
folding his sheep along a dust-veiled road.
Down by the thinned river,
someone's pain addresses us, but only he
dares to raise his eyes or to tumble his hands
                    in the foaming water.
His knowledge lies blood black and sun red

in spider lines, etched in his goat's hide folio,
where every morph of injury submits to his healing's syntax.
In my tomb, I hear his voice.
Now here, with one who follows me, I wallop
the cabaret-lit dimness of Luis Moya,
and step into the second water, rising perhaps
out of a deer's lair, hare's seat, bird's nest, or the grave.
I recall my curandero's virtue,
and the way he arranges his materia medica—
herb-laden, with creosote and Mormon tea,
lavender-starred white horse nettle, the sego lily bulb—
                                        before our eyes,
a cloud of flowers, from which the lily bursts,
and the echo of a blessing welcomes one
who has been embraced by Remedios.

Having no destination, we know we will arrive,
leaves blown down the back streets of night town,
pages from a scattered book
                          not even the night can read.
And yet,
            Within its depths I saw ingathered, bound by
            love in one volume,
the tobaquillo dance of my curandero,
and heard, at once, the hummingbird, whispering
                          in this bracero's voice,
felt prophetic notions in the hands filled with lilies.
This patron of travelers knows I will not perish
through secret things, and that my spirit
has walked out of a racially shattered house,
to find comfort in his likeness, challenge
                          in the book of his difference.
This saint's day opens a book I thought I had closed.
"And I, who never burned for my own vision more
than I do for his,"
find love the perfect vessel to trouble the waters.

32

SAN DIEGO (NOVEMBER 13TH)

At home, at this hour, the fog would just be braiding
the willows, and there would be time and light enough
to slip into the lake with gum boots and a light pole,
looking for breakfast.
                        Here, when the morning foghorn groans,
he can only dream of sea bass, or admire the tuna boats
                        scudding home with the catch.
Though his water life has gone, Jake always wakes
in a starched room, kicks off the night's heaviness,
                        and prays.
I call him son of Zebedee,
and reach for the thunder in his laugh.
His black sons search his blue eyes,
and call him Yacub, the wrong Jack of the common folk,
the quivering seajockey out of Lake Charles,
too dumb to know his uselessness, or his use.
They would have him beheaded, or have him wait
in the desert for some ghost's descent,
and, if I should confess how I, like him, wait
in my buffed room for a call in the night,
or for the ascent of veiled women,
poking with their staffs in the swamp ground around me,
I would be rewarded with their cold kiss of peace.

Jake walks his gum boots on Ford's car lot out on Pacific;
I flit my jitney around Todd's shipyards.
Pillars, perhaps, to those who depend upon us,
we return, in the evenings, to cold melons and silence,
and plot a slow escape down to Tijuana, in an old car
                        with wintry breath.
Our sons will not sit stiff in their beers, and listen
to two old men reconstruct the geography of sainthood.
Let them sleep.

I would turn left at San Diego, toward Imperial County,
and follow Mountain Spring rocks, with the Toltec and Maya
faces now reconceived in the rock face,
and the desert sky lit by Yucca elata, God's candles.
Back there, in San Pedro, something rides us
—memory of a white horse in a field, or of the ring
of a Spanish coin with the twin's face stamped upon it.
Only a crippled king—a lord lion, whose name threatens
to decompose and reappear, figured as the name of this city—
                              can save us.
I reach for the sweet seat of Pico, the Mountain Star,
or clutch at the Aztec urn and cross in San Diego's yard.
Surely, continents revolve on my brother's name,
and I invest him with the power to sit in judgment
on my shallow faith and the patience to wait
until compassion rises out of the many deaths
he left in the valley at Lake Charles.
Time now to compose love's epistle.
And for that I have waited, in my faith's confusion,
if only to be the scribe of the darkness by which we live.

The car moves slowly on.
Jake sits beside me,
his smile a radiance about him,
his silence a hant's song near the altar
                    from which a god has fled.

33

SANTA BÁRBARA (DECEMBER 4TH)

Who now takes an oath on the peacock, Hera's bird?
And who could depict that feast on Barbara's table?
The day the saint's father struck her, Ọya stripped and shivered
him in the earth, Hera's lightning sheared him,
and he became another exposed to sudden death,
subject to his daughter's care.

Jarena Lee feels the lightning in a psalm,
and thinks of dying,
returns to herself under the thunderclap of another text
that shows her her troubled heart,
and in that instant,
"as if a garment, which had entirely enveloped
my whole person . . . split at the crown of my head,"
and I could forgive *every* creature, and "tell of the wonders
and of the goodness of him who had clothed me with his
salvation."

> I exhort you, even though I ride
> only the broken buggy of my own conversion,
> and even though I think that no one will
> believe power's promise in my voice.
> Must I, like incorruptible Hera,
> cinch my husband's failings?
> or be the faithful wife
> and follow my man out of Ọyọ,
> become a river goddess only when he
> knows himself as a god?

Where does the crown sit,
being neither royal nor liturgical?
Why does it shine only in conquest and games?
I adorn my own with Graces and the Seasons,
and the cuckoo sits upon my scepter to remind me

of spring, and of love.
Every celebration now speaks of the power in love's form,
and the way a flowered diadem recalls my tubular beads
and the conviviality in plantains and beans and mashed corn.

Even so,
        "At a certain time, I was beset with the idea,
        that soon or late I should fall from grace,
        and lose my soul at last . . ."
But I know that I shall never return from the cross,
or that I shall return only when I have fashioned,
out of my own creative wood, the ship upon which
        I will write my real name.

This will be the hour of my redemption, a second blessing.
For death holds no promise.
And men who preach with my voice can only sanction my gift.
My gift is in the ceaseless journey from moment to moment,
from place to place, places given in dreams and clothed by the Spirit.
"But let it be remarked that [I] have never found that Spirit
to lead me contrary to the Scriptures of Truth."
Coco de mer, I lie with him, nourished by my vision,
set free by sailing away, and into,
                gold, silver, ivory, and peacocks.

NEW ENGLAND DAYS

34

THE WHITE DEER

The sun says she is there,
a dawn moon in a green field.

I imagine she came down,
riding the wooden horse ark;
or perhaps she was coiled within it,
and leapt from its serpent's embrace
when it lightly touched the earth.
But these are matters for a winter evening,
after the snow has been cleared,
and the thick docks of maple and birch
have been split and put away.
No need to resolve them now,
or to imagine that they are resolvable
without the enhanced water of the neighbors'
                    contemplation and resolve.
Before spring fully arrives,
we will all be thoroughly adept in her roots,
and able to hear her wet foot ripple the grass,
as she paddles from under the evergreens
                    into the clearing.

Night hunters seek her out.
I turn in the close air of my nightmares
because I hear their goose-voiced pickups
splash through the field's jade waves.
Those voices only serve to veil her.
                    And the light
the hunters cast in darkening circles
never seems to fix her white coat.

Deerjackers have the tail of things.
It would be better if they came,

disarmed and in awe,
when she feeds on withering apples
                    and fallen buds,
when the only sound in a crowd of seekers
is a common breathing,
or the hushed tale of a memory like prayer.

I have grown,
day by day, in my own regard,
and in the distinction her tranquility
                    brings to the field.
I have grown, even though it is she
who has taken the field I say I own.

Each day I mark her pilgrim's satisfaction
and the way she satisfies these other pilgrims.

I would be taken into the depths of her crossed bones,
to encounter the seed that gave her such an exact light,
and to spiral under that clairvoyance that taught her to bear
                    her body with such grace.

Danger lies in that grace.
Danger lies in the moment when the others have come
to understand the seed's white presence, in a body
that could father us without a hint of solace,
and induce us to dance out of the first dream,
into betrayal, and the word that takes its first step
                    into death.
Life here, I know, is a middle term,
breath arising from the arc and dimension
of a soul in wood, and the wood within a sheltered wood,
being a desert design, winding
          toward a new moon in a green field.

Night must fall upon your rosary of explanation.

Now, a man,
who has made himself intimate with the night,
sits, camouflaged, in a tree, and aims
his silent magnum at the white deer.

35

All through a bitter April,
spring has refused our invitation.
Still, the inner seasons turn,
and, when the ice breaks
and the blue water furs white
over the rocks in small streams,
the silence that had blanketed itself
in the crippled apple tree
                              walks away.

I hear that silence in the water
when I stand on the pond's edge,
and watch my father brace himself
in the stocks of his fish house
out on the ice, a silence
that seems a loon weariness,
a burden of lost bear,
lately moaning coyotes cutting
through the sheep's straw fur,
                              for the kill.

Over the ridge now, I see morning
rise in white smoke over white houses,
and know the cows have awakened
to their milky certainties.
I awaken to the depth charge of my own
stove's fire, having dreamed all night
of the smoky weeds lying deep in the pond
and the past certainties of mid-May,
when a blaze of dandelions lit my path
                              to the water.

Spring's reasons come hard through the trunk of winter.

A father like mine can spend too long in a mind's ditch,
filled with paper potatoes, curdled cabbage, squash
and zucchini blooming in floods;
                              can huddle too long
with death's gazette, chimney fires, a son's leaving,
a barn gone down under heavy snow.
I would awaken the water's flow in winter,
and have him uncoil in his boat,
with the peppery summer wind tugging at his laziness.
That would be more than the sap of April's promise,
less than April's refusal.

Mid-May.
I grow impatient with the lazy sting of blackflies,
with the patient way my neighbors snuffle
in their gardens and gauze them for the cold nights,
with the loggers' bourbon legends, and with the clouds
down from Canada spread-eagled over treetops.
"Something the heart here misses."
But wise old Indian Pond erupts on the left hand of spring.
In the sand at its feet,
someone, borrowing the incense and fire of another life,
has cut a crescent moon, to mark the place
where tethered April broke
                              and disappeared.

36

The poplars have grown their winter cotton,
snow that winds a shaggy warmth around the branches.
At night now, even when the moon has tucked itself
into its patchy quilt,
you can go from this house in the hollow
to the house at the point of the stone wall,
following the trees' light and silence
through fog that inexplicably rises
                              and suddenly disappears.
White seams in the lapis lazuli skirt of a New
Hampshire night remind us of the first time
we saw the aluminum shimmy of northern lights,
the hants' tree houses,
from which, through the fluttering doors,
we expected to hear an hechicera voice
and the montuno of a home we had swiftly
                              abandoned.

There is another voice,
high in the White Mountains,
one we carried in your father's urn
from appleless Jersey and scattered
in the moss shadow of a singular apple tree.
In spring,
it comes in the white-throated sparrow's song,
a melisma of misery tempered by the thrill of survival.

Soon, the mauve summer sky
will strike its evening tympanum,
and move you through the deep waters of wonder
                              into a forgiving sleep.

SOURCES AND ROOTS

37

Ayer me habló el corazón,
y su pena me contó,
llorando; so I lie doggó
in the skirts of a cantina known
for the quality of hearts bled
on its Moorish tiles; style, my man,
undoes the grandest among us.
But listen, whatever the fuss,
the story will be taken in hand
by the keeper of my cups and read
by charros polishing the mine-
cut diamonds of a grief so
fertile that water lilies flow
on desert sands, greenly windblown
by love's fortunate demise. Crone-
wily skill might give me a bow
to sling and round couplets to sow
under cherry trees, though I have flown
with mynah birds, and they have shown
the arc of your love's flight, the low
trajectory of escape. No,
cosas de Catalonia son,
paschal lacerations. ¡Merced!,
peacocks toward an open hand
swim, swerve, ride their calamitous
mother love—hope that sustains us
through dawn's late tumult and command
of pearlish fevers which have led
hearts astray, seen them overthrown
when they were ready to bestow
themselves upon one's grace. I know
what this spent heart has left alone.

38

Un siglo de auscencia might,
when the axe bites the ceiba tree,
matter; two fast-moving rats, three
kola nuts, an Iroko light,—
business for the domestic bird—
a blessing, one by one—I live
on flowering water and give
you penny songs, by which the surd
of a fallen flower raises
hope in me. Such penny phrases
have lit a Oaxaca morning,
love's very rim-fire adorning
the humillación of falling
away from flowers, the galling
remembrance of a hill bereft
of turtledoves. If only deft
Tlacahuepan would offer me
his skimpy sun to enchant, free
of his dolens nature, his crest-
ed heart might sing us to our rest.
Un siglo de ausencia, night
fails to find you here and I see
my loss has now become the lee
side of my heart, mask of delight,
encumbrance upon the one word
Náhuatl songs do not forgive,
or speak, when they serve a deliv-
erance the tempered heart has heard.

39

Dime en donde encontrar-
te, disposable heart, red star
by which I set my course and flow,
a vessel marked by the dim glow
of pride. I am a song that cleaves
to its Guinea way, stops, deceives
itself, falls through a lowered tone
and returns, enhanced by its own
failure, to the key it sustains.
Not one word in this song constrains
my delight in you, or tells me
why, that without you, I am free
from pain, bereft of clemency,
or how the domestic bird, sea-
wise and durable, can inspire
the yellow feather of desire.
A plumed Huasteca feather bed
kept my floating spirit dry, wed
me to lilies that would soon wither
in Xochimilco, the slither-
ing sound of the dead in my ear.
I have come upon my own bier,
deep in the soft spur of your eyes,
though I know your ransom denies
me passion's hobbyhorse, the same
voice that ancianas use to flame
the wine bowl, in which my name
blossoms, floats, furls, and dies. They shame
me with the easy way they ride
love's sepulchre, the way they hide
compassion in a mother's sleeve.
No one has taught me how to weave
the green threads of the sparrow's song;
in motion, my voice takes the wrong
turn, becomes a syllogismus,

contradance of an ambitus,
embodied and redeemed. Now all
the versions of love's death enthrall
and enable me to recall
light that shrouds us in its slow fall.

CODA

I

Esta tierra da de todo.
Oh, perhaps, you will see no sloe
plum, or no white-tailed, ginger doe,
break-dancing at sunset when snow
shows us its blackberry wine skin.
But you will never see a thin-
ly dressed table, or be distressed
by a forged love. Here, you are blessed.

II

Council houses turn gray faces
south, Andalucian traces
being perhaps on someone's mind.
Your mind is on the color blind-
ness that led you to draw this moor
heat about your shoulders, a poor
shawl against the withering kiss
of absence, timeless, returning bliss.

III

Without your dead, faith dies, and one
learns how the extensible sun
of belief and aspiration
serve such an exhilaration
that only faith in love allows.
So even that pine can arouse
your suman heart, call spirit's rain
into the heat of your domain.
>Químbara cosongo,
>Químbara cosongo,
>Químbara cosongo. . . .

Princeton Series of Contemporary Poets